IF SHARKS DISAPPEARED

Lily Williams

WAYLAND
www.waylandbooks.co.uk

THIS IS A HEALTHY OCEAN. It's a balanced environment where many different animals and plants thrive. The ocean is home to a lot of creatures —
big,
small,
slimy,
cute and ...

... SCARY.

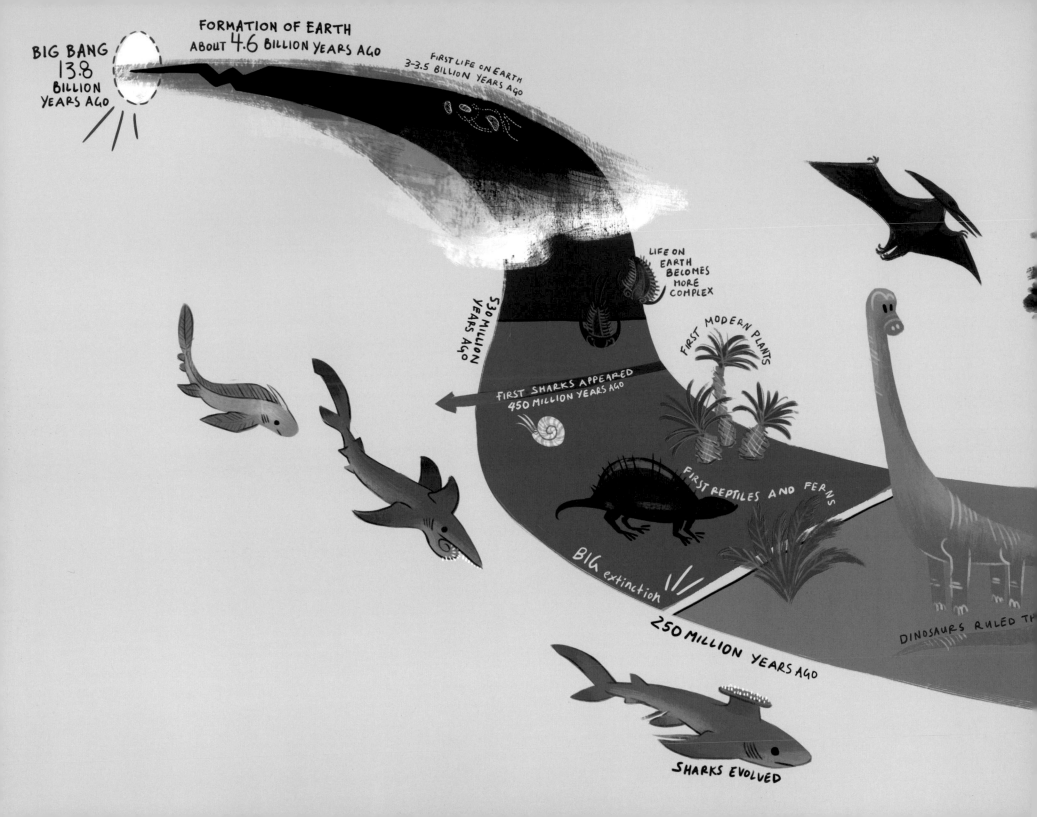

BIG BANG 13.8 BILLION YEARS AGO

FORMATION OF EARTH ABOUT 4.6 BILLION YEARS AGO

FIRST LIFE ON EARTH 3-3.5 BILLION YEARS AGO

LIFE ON EARTH BECOMES MORE COMPLEX

530 MILLION YEARS AGO

FIRST SHARKS APPEARED 450 MILLION YEARS AGO

FIRST MODERN PLANTS

FIRST REPTILES AND FERNS

BIG extinction

250 MILLION YEARS AGO

DINOSAURS RULED TH

SHARKS EVOLVED

Sharks have helped keep our oceans balanced for about 450 million years. Over that time, they evolved into the more than 400 different species that exist today.

TALL TREES MADE FORESTS

FIRST MODERN MAMMALS

FIRST GRASSLANDS

TODAY!

HUMANS APPEARED 200,000 YEARS AGO

LOTS OF DIFFERENT DINOS

Mass extinction

60-65 MILLION YEARS AGO

MODERN SHARKS

Sharks are apex predators, which means they are at
the top of the food chain in their ecosystem, the ocean.
Losing an apex predator species can cause devastating
effects in an environment.

Today, roughly a quarter of shark species are at risk of extinction due to overfishing. What could happen if this continues and sharks disappear altogether?

If sharks disappeared ...

... the ocean would no longer be balanced. Although different species have different diets, most sharks typically eat sick, slow or weak prey, leaving the healthy animals to reproduce. If sharks disappeared ...

... the populations of seals, sea lions
and walruses would potentially explode.

At higher populations,
they would eat more and
more fish, and eventually,

once there weren't any fish left,

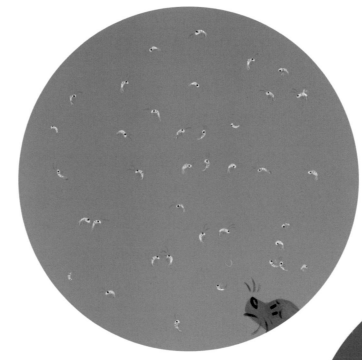

they'd starve and die out, as well.

If fish, seals, sea lions and
walruses disappeared ...

... plankton, which is what many fish that are lower on the food chain eat, could quickly grow out of control. That could make the ocean a thick sludge. Nothing could survive in this water. If the ocean became unlivable ...

... many species of land animal that rely on the ocean for food, such as seabirds and polar bears, could starve and die out.

The loss of those animals could cause still more species further inland to die out.

This pattern of cause and effect, called a trophic cascade, could spread like a wave across countries and continents until animals around the globe were affected, from bees, to birds, to bears and eventually to ...

... US.

All species depend on one another to survive by keeping our planet's ecosystems in balance. And luckily, today ...

... sharks still exist.

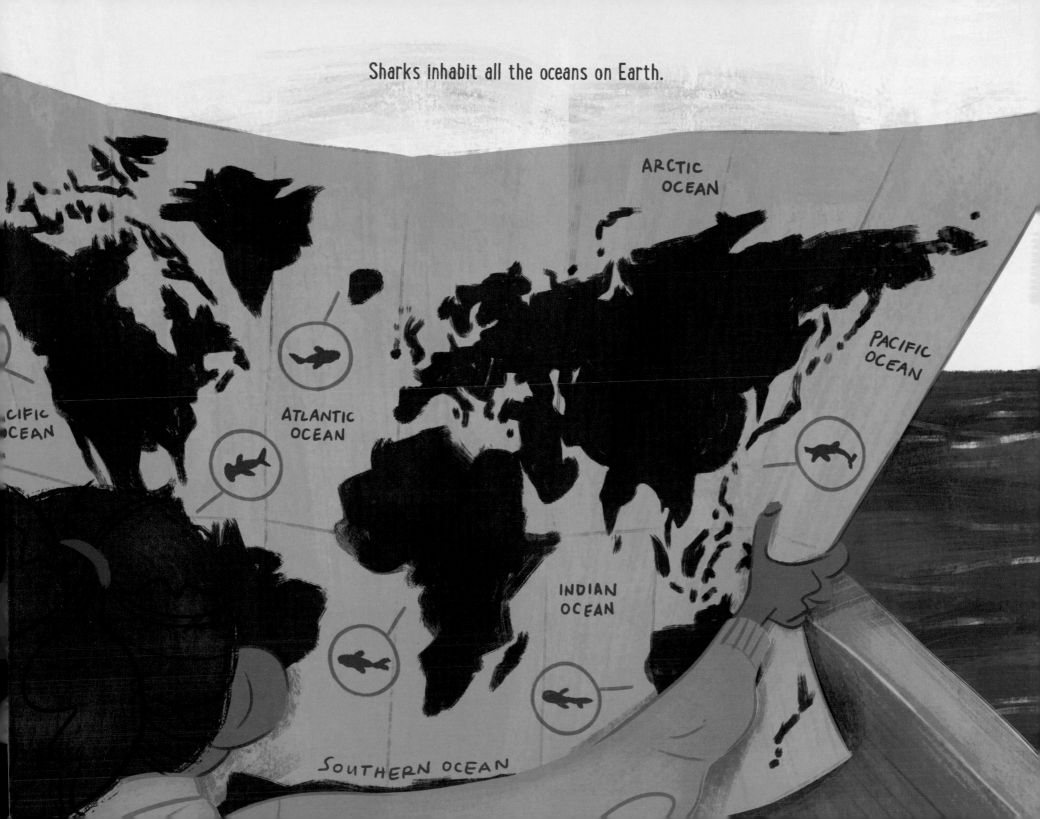

Sharks inhabit all the oceans on Earth.

If we remember that we are all connected and if we work together, sharks — and our whole planet as we know it — will thrive. And maybe we'll see that what once seemed so scary ...

... isn't so scary after all.

GLOSSARY

APEX PREDATOR: the top predator in a food chain.

BALANCE: when populations are at levels that allow all species to exist in harmony.

BIG BANG: most astronomers believe that the Universe began with a huge explosion, called the Big Bang, about 13.8 billion years ago, when a single point expanded and created space, time and matter.

CARTILAGE: the tough, flexible living material that makes up much of a shark's skeleton. It is much lighter than bone.

ECOSYSTEM: all the living things, plants and animals, which live in a particular area or environment.

ENVIRONMENT: all the living and non-living things (rocks, air etc.) on Earth, or in one part of the planet.

EVOLUTION: the process of change over a long period of time due to natural selection.

EXTINCTION: when a species, or a population of an animal or plant, dies out completely.

FOOD CHAIN: the way all animals get energy by eating each other or eating plants. In the ocean food chain, the primary producers are sea plants, such as tiny plant plankton and seaweed, which make their own food using energy from the Sun. They are eaten by the primary consumers (krill, small fish, tiny shrimps), which are eaten by the secondary consumers (bigger fish, seals, sea lions, dolphins), which are also called predators. The top predators in an ocean food chain (many sharks, killer whales, humans) eat the secondary consumers (smaller predators).

NATURAL SELECTION: the very slow process by which a species adapts to its environment over many generations, making it easier for future generations to thrive. This occurs when individuals with the best characteristics survive and breed, while less well-suited individuals do not.

OVERFISHING: catching so many fish from a particular ocean or sea that the adult fish cannot breed fast enough to replenish the population.

PLANKTON: very small plants that live in water that are the primary producers in the ocean food chain. Some plankton are zooplankton, tiny animals that eat the plant plankton, such as krill.

Rabbits 3-5 million years ago ⟶ Rabbits today!

SPECIES: a group of living things (animals or plants) that can breed together to produce young or offspring which in turn can reproduce, such as humans, whale sharks or giraffes.

SHARK FIN SOUP: a traditional Chinese or Vietnamese soup served on special occasions, such as at weddings. Although the soup is considered a luxury item, it has become quite popular, and large numbers of sharks are killed just for their fins. Sometimes sharks are released alive after having their fins cut off, but they almost always die from blood loss or because they can't swim properly.

THRIVE: to grow well and succeed.

TROPHIC CASCADE: the chain of events that happens once a top predator is removed from or added to an ecosystem. These events can cause changes in the populations of all the other animals in the environment and dramatically shift the whole ecosystem, affecting other predators, prey and nutrient levels.

SHARKS ARE IN TROUBLE

An estimated 100 million sharks are killed every year. Most of them are used to make shark fin soup, a Chinese/Vietnamese delicacy. Though shark fins have no taste or nutritional value, they can be sold for a lot of money. Sharks are also killed for their teeth, jaws, livers, skin and cartilage. These parts are used in dietary supplements, skincare products, cosmetics and leather goods. Non-selective fishing methods like netting, trawling (where a boat drags a net through the water or along the ocean floor), and longlining (where one main fishing line dangles many smaller lines with hooks) also kill large numbers of sharks. Sometimes people even kill sharks out of fear, thinking that having fewer of them in the oceans will keep people safer in the water. So many sharks are killed that roughly one-quarter of species are now under threat of extinction. The truth is, people are more likely to be killed by a disease-carrying mosquito, a cow, a vending machine, a horse, a bee sting or falling off their bed than they are to be killed by a shark.

HOW YOU CAN HELP SAVE SHARKS

You can help save sharks by being a conscious consumer:

- Don't buy products containing shark in any form, such as shark fin soup, shark squalene (shark liver oil), or shark teeth, jaws or cartilage.
- Buy only fish that were caught sustainably, which means that not too many fish were caught at one time or in a way that harmed the ocean environment. Look for the blue fish symbol of the Marine Stewardship Council and check out the seafood guides on the World Wide Fund for Nature website (WWF).
- Stay up-to-date on news about sharks and know what laws are being passed.
- Tell your local MP or local government representative you want better protection of sharks and marine life. Let them know you support more regulation of fishing practices for the fishing industry.
- Travel to, or learn more about, places that support shark education, like South Africa, Australia's Great Barrier Reef and Baie Ternay Marine National Park in Seychelles.
- Support causes that look after sharks. Get involved with local and global shark advocacy programs, or start one of your own. Tell your friends about the plight of sharks and encourage them to make sustainable changes in their lives.
- Create shark art!

AUTHOR'S NOTE

The information in this book is a simplified description of a complex process.
To learn more, start with the books and websites listed at the bottom of this page.

I love sharks. I love to read about them, research them and look at photos of them. I kept hearing that sharks are necessary to our world, but it wasn't always explained *why* that was. I decided to look into it, and what I found were scientific studies and speculations.

So I decided to show why our world needs sharks. The information in this book is based on the best research available and on opinions and explanations from esteemed scientists. While some of the information is just educated guesses about what might happen, those guesses reflect what marine scientists have learned during years of studying the oceans. There is no way to predict the future, but looking to the past can help us understand the impact we could have. And we know for certain that all species are in some way connected and rely on one another to survive and thrive. I hope that this book will inspire you to care about one of our world's fiercest animals and to find ways you can help protect our oceans. Let's save sharks!

ACKNOWLEDGEMENTS

This book would not have been possible without the following people, who assisted me in my research and encouraged my exploration: Minju Chang of BookStop Literary Agency, who took a chance on me and supported my work tirelessly; Emily Feinberg of Roaring Brook Press, who believed in me from day one; Elizabeth Clark, who took everything to the next level; John E. McCosker, Ph.D., Chair Emeritus of Aquatic Biology at California Academy of Sciences, who advised me with kindness and encouraged me; and David McGuire, director of Shark Stewards, who introduced me to so much. To them all, I am deeply indebted.

FIND OUT MORE: BOOKS AND WEBSITES

The Variety of Life by Nicola Davies and Lorna Scobie (Hodder Children's Books, 2017)
Mega Shark by Gary Jeffrey (Franklin Watts, 2017)
If You Were a Shark by Clare Hibbert (Franklin Watts, 2013)
Surprising Sharks by Nicola Davies (Walker, 2008)

The World Wide Fund for Nature website includes seafood guides, helping you to choose the right fish to buy and eat: **wwf.panda.org/how_you_can_help/live_green/out_shopping/seafood_guides/**

The Sealife Trust's website offers tips on how everyone can help combat overfishing of the world's oceans: **www.sealifetrust.org/What-we-do/Combating-Overfishing**

Explore the Australian Marine Conservation Society website to learn about conservation and the marine environment: **www.marineconservation.org.au/pages/learn.html**

Discover more information about sharks on the Shark Trust website: **www.sharktrust.org/en/about_sharks**

ANGEL & MONK
SHARKS

FRILLED & GILLED
SHARKS

SPINY & LANTERN
SHARKS

HORN SHARKS